PRO GAMER

PRESENTS

THE DEFINITIVE GUIDE TO FORTNITE 2022

A TOTALLY INDEPENDENT PUBLICATION

Written by Naomi Berry
Designed by Chris Dalrymple

PBR

A Pillar Box Red Publication

© 2021. Published by Pillar Box Red Publishing Limited. Printed in the EU.

ISBN 978-1-912456-94-9

Images © Epic Games.

WELCOME

It's safe to say that if there were ever a nuclear razing of the planet, Fortnite would be right beside those cockroaches as the world's final survivors... and Fortnite might just beat those roaches out in the long run.

Bear in mind that it's usual fare for online games to blaze bright and then burn out like a shooting star; Fortnite, however, has continued hurtling towards us with increasing speed and power like the Season 10 meteor that reset the game with Chapter 2. Since its Battle Royale debut in 2017, Fortnite has continued to grow and grow, and the last year was arguably its biggest - foraying into mainstream media more so than ever before (be it in collaboration with global juggernaut Marvel Universe, or making headlines by taking Apple head on).

Fortnite has done more than stand the test of time - it's beyond that now. The game isn't going anywhere anytime soon. And while it may arguably be the most popular game in the world (and as certain as death and taxes at this point), Epic Games isn't taking anything for granted; there's always new updates and new content ready to keep players on their toes, with the latest updates bringing the biggest changes to gameplay the game has seen since its release.

This guide is perfect for all sorts of players, from newbies to vets. There's no one way to succeed in Fortnite. The game constantly keeps things fresh, so learning the basic gameplay elements and mechanics is the best foundation you can have to develop your own playstyle and craft a path to clinch that Battle Royale.

Best be prepared -
there's a storm coming.

CONTENTS

GLOSSARY

One of the reasons Fortnite has managed to hang around for so long has been its ability to become more than just a one-round game; it's become a virtual world in itself, with its very own language. Sure, if you've played a Battle Royale game before, you may be familiar with some of these terms, but there's a lexicon unique to Fortnite that you best have mastered if you want to communicate effectively in voice chat and be competitive.

Like all languages, you'll definitely pick some of it up as you go. But there's no harm in a quick review in advance for that head start, or at least to keep as reference if your teammate hits you with "LeBron's House" and leaves you stumped.

ADS:

ADS stands for Aim Down Sights, which is when you can 'zoom' in on your shot for increased accuracy. This can be done by using your right mouse click.

AFK:

AFK stands for Away From Keyboard, and is used to describe inactive players.

BAIT:

Totally unrelated to fishing, despite its recent boom in-game - 'bait' is used here in the verb form, and refers to luring a player into a dangerous situation. Be suspicious if you stumble across a huge pile of loot on the ground - there may be another player bush camping nearby waiting to take their shot.

BIG POT:

A common term used to refer to the Rare Shield Potion.

BLOOM:

A weapon's bloom is the spray of its bullets once fired. Weapons with bloom fire bullets anywhere within their crosshairs, which means a lower accuracy compared to a direct snipe. You can lessen bloom by either crouching or standing still while firing.

THE BUBBLE:

The area of the map unaffected by the storm.

BUSH CAMPER:

A player that uses bushes to take cover and hide.

BM:

This stands for 'Bad Manners', and generally refers to post-win or post-kill behaviour at the opponent's expense (like, say, doing the electro shuffle on top of their fresh corpse).

BOT:

Someone who is playing poorly, making questionable gameplay decisions.

DOWNED/KNOCKED:

A player whose HP has been depleted but they haven't been fully eliminated yet.

FULL SEND/RUSH:

To go all in, aggressive; a full out assault.

HEALS:

Any item that provides health points, from bandages to fish.

HOT DROP:

A popular landing spot, usually a Point of Interest.

LAUNCH:

Generally used to refer to launch pads.

LEBRON'S HOUSE:

A house with a basketball court attached.

LOADOUT:

The weapons and items you collect across the match. Having an ideal loadout in mind will speed up the loot and cop-or-drop decision making process.

MATS:

Mats is shorthand for materials, i.e. wood, brick and metal.

MINIS:

Generally used to refer to the Small Shield Potion.

NO SCOPE:

Shooting an accurate shot with a sniper rifle without using the weapon's scope.

ONE/ONE-SHOT:

If an opponent is 'One' or 'One-Shot', then they are one shot away from being eliminated. This is vital for communication as it lets teammates know whether to rush an enemy or take cover.

POI:

An acronym for Point of Interest, referring to notable locations on the map like Retail Row, Lazy Lake etc.

PVE:

Player versus Environment. This is a newer element in Battle Royale, with the addition of hostile AI in matches.

PVP:

Player versus Player.

REZ:

Short for Resurrection, a request from players to their teammates to resurrect them.

SHIELD POP:

This call means an opponent's shield has been damaged or destroyed.

SPAWN ISLAND:

The area you are loaded into before boarding the Battle Bus to the main island. You cannot access this part of the map once the game has begun.

THE 3 BASICS:
GATHERING

When it comes to clinching that Battle Royale victory, there are three basic skill sets you want to master: gathering, building and surviving. Let's dive into the first, and perhaps most fundamental - gathering. Gathering is the foundation - quite literally, because it's integral to actual building, and building is integral to navigating the map, controlling the flow of battles and ultimately being the last one standing.

TRUSTY TOOLS

When you land on the island, it's with naught but your glider and your trusty pickaxe. While it can be used as a weapon, it's about as effective as a potent sneeze with only 20 damage per hit, so it's best used for the purpose it was made for: harvesting.

For the most efficient harvesting, aim your pickaxe at the Critical Point: this blue circle marks the weakest point of the target, and striking it increases both the yield and the speed.

KNOW YOUR MATS

Materials (or "mats", as they're commonly called) can be easily sorted into three categories: wood, stone and metal.

TIP:

You can harvest up to x999 pieces of each material in Battle Royale (and x500 in Arena), so don't be shy when it comes to stocking up. It's better to be with than without, especially for those end-game duels.

WOOD

Wood is the most common mat, and while it's the easiest material to find and fastest to build with, keep in mind that it's also the weakest. It can be found in abundance across the island, and can be harvested from sources such as:

- **Trees and Bushes:** These are found all across the map, but best head to an orchard area if you want to max out quickly. Remember, pros never chop the tree down in its entirety - check out p. 36-37 for more info!

- **Furniture:** An easy quick resource if you land in a residential hot spot and are making your exit through a house.

- **Wooden Structures:** From fences and shacks to boxes and crates (and sometimes even cacti). There's a good chance if you strike anything on the island, it'll glean wood.

TIP:

You can also find mats within Chests, Supply Drops and Loot Llamas.

STONE

Stone is the true mats middleman; it's the second strongest and the second fastest. To find stone, look no further than:

- **Rocks and Boulders:** You can usually find decent boulders near water, and also in the quarry like areas around Fatal Fields.

- **Walls:** Sometimes you've got to tear through those houses you land in if you need to up your inventory. They're not the fastest to pull down though, so don't rely on these if you're in a rush or find yourself with unexpected company.

TIP:

It's generally harder to find mats the longer you survive, so it's better to stock up at the beginning of the match with the intention of saving it for later.

METAL

Metal is the strongest of the three mats, but that fortitude comes with a trade-off: it's by far the slowest to build with. While it may not be ideal for those high speed build battles, it's value lies in hunkering down and providing the best cover if you need to turtle and recover. It's a little harder to find than the other resources, but you can harvest it from:

- **Vehicles:** Vehicles are the obvious go to, but they run the risk of triggering alarms that might alert enemies to your position, so be wary.

- **Metal Structures:** Usually in the form of trailers, keep an eye out for these around Dirty Docks for a quick metal boost.

THE 3 BASICS:
BUILDING

With our knowledge of basic mats down, it's time to move onto the next basic in Fortnite mastery: building. Building is the truly unique element that allows Fortnite to stand out from the increasingly crowded Battle Royale genre, and while you can certainly try to play without it, it certainly makes things a lot easier if you at least have the fundamentals down.

Look, we get it: building in Fortnite can be pretty intimidating. You watch a pro on their stream get into it with an enemy and they're racing up towers built in a flash and in the time you blink, they've cornered their foe, boxed them in, dropped a trap on them and are somehow already twenty stories down on their exit. It can be a lot to digest.

But no one's expecting that from you - building is just as useful a way for you to manipulate the map to better cater to your win conditions. Caught in the storm? Build a tower and launchpad to glide off the top for faster travel out. On the run in difficult terrain? Build a path between mountain peaks beneath your feet. Stumbled into an unwanted battle? Build cover and secure an exit. Grab your blueprint and your pencil - let's get down to the basics of building.

PUT IT IN TURBO

If you want to master building, then Turbo Build is a must. This configuration allows you to hold left-click and build continuously via aim. Make sure it's enabled in your settings if you're on PC, but if you're using a controller, then switch the config to Builder Pro.

Material	Structure	Min HP	Max HP	Until Max HP (sec)
Wood	Wall	90	150	4
Wood	Ramp, Floor, Roof	84	140	3.5
Stone	Wall	99	300	11.5
Stone	Ramp, Floor, Roof	93	280	12
Metal	Wall	110	500	24.5
Metal	Ramp, Floor, Roof	101	460	22.5

NUMBERS, NUMBERS, NUMBERS

Like most things in Fortnite, mats have stats, and these stats are important to understand before you start throwing up towers to the sky.

TIP:

Each structure costs 10 mats from your inventory to construct.

So what do these numbers mean in real time? Pretty easy: wood is weak but the fastest to use for emergencies (like a quick escape or negating fall damage), and metal is best for long term/late game structures. As for stone? It's not the best or worst at anything, so ultimately will never be your first pick.

THE IMPORTANCE OF FOUNDATION

Just like real world structures, the importance of foundation is integral to Fortnite builds. You can build the wackiest, far-leaning, far-reaching

masterpiece - but it's got to be anchored to the map at some point in order to stand. This is key to remember both offensively and defensively: if you take out the foundation, the whole thing will come crashing down.

- So when it comes to building your own structures, be sure to use more than one anchor. More targets for enemies to take down means more time for you to get up and out of there.

- And if you're fighting someone who has a built high ground advantage on you, don't waste time trying to snipe them from the ground; seek out the building's anchor and bring the fight down to you.

- And hey, if you see two people already engaged in a build fight, why not seize the opportunity to strike down their foundations and send them crashing down? They likely didn't see you coming due to being preoccupied, and if they haven't already worn down each other's HP, there's a good chance the fall damage and slight disorientation might be tipping the scales in your favour.

TIP:

You can also build against cliffs, mountains, hills and sides of pre-existing buildings for extra structural support. Your structure can be anchored anywhere on the terrain - it doesn't have to be just the ground.

KNOW YOUR STRUCTURES

There are four types of structures that you can build:

- **Walls:** The wall is your best defensive structure, your quick fix when you find yourself under fire. You can also build this pre-emptively before a fight and edit in some vantage points for shooting.

- **Floors:** Floors come in handy during map traversal when you want to cut across an open area, or to put beneath you to provide cover from below when you're in a duel.

- **Ramps:** The ramp is great for mobility, as it can allow you to gain the high ground during a duel, or reach parts of the map you wouldn't otherwise be able to on foot.

- **Roofs:** The roof is a rarer build, and best used to box in opponents during a build duel, or to provide cover from above if you're hunkering down on the low ground.

Of course, there's more to it than simply learning four structures. Every creator knows that half of the work is the editing process, and Fornite's no exception. Responsive edits to your builds depending on the context is a surefire way to climb the ranks - add a door for a quick exit, a window for a new vantage point, or even a hole in the floor for a sudden drop ambush. Keep adapting your build as you read the situation.

YOUR GO-TO BUILDS

Sure, there are no limits to what you can create with the build mechanic, but recreating your take on the Guggenheim is definitely something best kept for Creative. For Battle Royale, efficiency is the name of the game, and there are four bread and butter builds to master for that competitive edge.

TIP:

But Creative and Battle Lab aren't just for would-be architects to flex - they're a great place to practice your Battle Royale builds without the pressure of opponents interrupting you with a headshot. Remember: practice makes perfect.

- **1x1:** A Fortnite builder's most basic of structures, the 1x1 is made of four walls, with a ramp in the middle for more integrity. The best way to build these is ramp first, then place surrounding walls with a quick spin.

- **Turtle:** A turtle is a 1x1 with a roof added, and while that doesn't sound all that impressive, just wait until you start building them next to each other and editing a path through them. Your opponent will have a tough time infiltrating them. They're a strong defensive option to go for if you're stuck on low ground, but they require quick fingers (particularly with editing) to pull off effectively.

- **Ramp Rush:** A regular ramp is easy enough, but as it's only one-layer, it's super easy to take down. Instead, opt for a Ramp Rush, which is basically a reinforced ramp, with a wall built beneath each incline. There's a stronger version of this, which also adds a floor (meaning there are three pieces to each individual incline). Both the 2- and 3-layered methods of building just mean your ramp is a lot sturdier, so your ascent is less likely to be interrupted by someone being able to destroy it.

- **90s:** The toughest nut to crack - the 90 isn't easy, by any means, but it sure is useful to have in your arsenal. The name comes from the countless 90 degree turns you'll need to make in order to throw one up: build a ramp and a wall, jump and turn 90 degrees, build a ramp and a wall, jump and turn 90 degrees... You get the drift. It's a pain to learn but they're by far the fastest way to gain relatively sturdy height, particularly in duels.

THE 3 BASICS:
SURVIVING - HEALTH AND SHIELDS

While there's one way to gather and one way to build, the last of the three basic skills - survival - is more multifaceted. To survive in Fortnite, there are three major elements you have to familiarize yourself with: weaponry, wildlife and (perhaps the most fundamental) health and shields.

So let's jump in with the core survival mechanic - your health and your shields. When it comes to Battle Royale, it's just as important to keep an eye on your own status as it is to have it on other players. After all, you don't get eliminated for not having the right weapons or not being able to aim - you get eliminated for running out of health.

RESTORING HP

BANDAGES:
Bandages are the most basic form of healing and while limited in their scope, they're definitely the most effective to use in a pinch. They heal 15 HP and have a 3 second usage time, but they have a healing cap of 75 HP.

MEDKIT:
The Medkit is a much stronger healing item, giving a full 100 HP boost. However, that HP comes at a cost, as it takes a full 10 seconds to consume. These are best used post-fight when you're sure you're safe or have adequate cover/distance.

COZY CAMPFIRE:

Environmental campfires can be found in different locations across the map, and provide free healing. It burns for 25 seconds and heals 2 HP per second to all nearby players, but you can relight the fire with pieces of wood if you want to go another round.

TIP:

If you're working in a duo or squad, then multi-target healing is your most effective option post-battle. There are usually options other than the Cozy Campfire - they usually circle in-and-out of the Vault, like the Chug Cannon and Bandage Bazooka.

RESTORING SHIELDS

The blue bar represents your shield, which protects your HP by absorbing any damage taken until it depletes to zero. Acquiring a shield should be in your top 3 priorities upon landing (alongside finding a weapon and keeping mobile), and you should be constantly trying to top it up throughout the match.

SMALL SHIELD POTION:

Small Shield Potions (sometimes referred to as Minis) grant 25 Shield Points, to a maximum of 50. While they can't give you a full Shield, their super fast usage time (only 2 seconds) makes them ideal to pop in a fight to recover damage taken.

SHIELD POTION:

Shield Potions (sometimes referred to as Big Pots) grant 50 Shield Points, up to the full shield maximum of 100. They take 5 seconds to consume, so are better used when alone or with strong cover and distance mid-fight.

FORAGING FOOD

Foraging food was introduced back in Season 4 and is still going strong. While you can't exactly rely solely on fresh produce to keep you up, it does certainly provide just the right amount to top up when you stumble across them, and sometimes even provides a little bonus boost too.

APPLE:

Apples provide 5 HP, and can be found in clusters near trees, like the Orchard.

BANANA:

Like apples, bananas also provide 5 HP. You can find them near palm trees along the coast.

CABBAGE:

Eat your greens, kids; cabbages give 10 HP. They can be found near farmland, and also in places like Retail Row.

COCONUT:

Mind your head when striking down palm trees, as these guys might drop down. They grant 5 HP, or 5 Shield Points if the user's HP is already full.

CORN:

Corn grants 10 HP, and can be found when destroying crops.

MUSHROOM:

Mushrooms are super useful because they provide 5 Shield Points, and since they have no cap, you can keep guzzling them until your Shield is full. You can usually find them in swampy areas and forests, growing in the shade.

PEPPER:

Peppers only give 5 HP but their main benefit is a 20% boost to your movement speed for 60 seconds.

SLURPHSROOM:

Slurpshrooms are an in-world genetic mutation of the regular mushroom that grants 10 HP/Shield Points. These grow exclusively in swampland.

If you're lucky, you may just stumble across a Produce Box (thanks, NOMS) in any of the POIs. Produce Boxes are like ammo boxes, but are filled with foraged fruits and vegetables for you to chow down on.

TIP:

Foraged food cannot be stored in your inventory, and have to be consumed when you find them.

TIP:

With the introduction of wildlife in Chapter 2: Season 6, you can also consume animal meat to heal 15 HP. It's a rare foraged item because it can be stored in your inventory.

FISHING

Fishing was introduced with Chapter 2 and is bigger and better than ever, with a whole new slew of underwater creatures to catch and consume to benefit the player. While some may be quick to turn their nose up at swapping out their gun for a fishing rod, it's actually proven to be a super useful mechanic, and definitely worth the (minimal, at best) trouble.

So what's the big deal with fishing? Well, fish are pretty good at keeping you topped up - maybe even better than actual healing items. On top of that, they only take 1 second to consume, which puts them on par with foraged foods as the quickest consumables, but with way more gain. Be sure to check out Fishing 101 on p. 30-33 for a deeper dive into fishing and their healing properties.

TIP:

Knowing what healing items are out on the field is integral to anyone looking to be on top of their game. It's wise to always check out patch notes each time Epic drops a new season to see what restorative items are in play.

THE 3 BASICS:
SURVIVING - WILDLIFE

We're deep into Chapter 2 and the island is more alive than it's ever been. It's not just fellow players out there with you anymore. Since the arrival of Season 6, the island has been teeming with wildlife - some ready to augment your loadout, and others prime to end your existence.

There's a whole spectrum of weird and wonderful wildlife out there, but not all are out to get you. You've got two options when it comes to animals:

- **Hunt 'Em:** Hunting wildlife gleans Crafting materials for weaponry. Most animals will drop an amount of Animal Bones or Meat when killed. For more information on Crafting weapons, check out p. 24-25.

- **Tame 'Em:** Certain wildlife can be tamed in two ways - either by crafting the Hunter's Cloak, or enticing them with meat or vegetables.

WELCOME TO THE WILD

There are a variety of animals you can come across on the island, ranging in size and ferocity from 0 to 100.

CHICKENS

Type	Location	HP
Passive	Near farms, corn fields	60

Chickens are totally harmless and serve as a great resource for some Crafting materials. If you pick up a chicken and jump, you'll hover (like a certain green-clad Hylian). Holding a chicken prevents fall damage, unless another player snipes it straight out of your hands.

FROGS

Type	Location	HP
Passive	Riverside, near water	20

Like chickens, frogs pose zero threat to you, and are an excellent resource for Crafting materials. Hunting frogs will give you Stink Sacs, which you need for the Primal Stink Bow. They're pretty evasive, so try to shoot them out from a distance instead of getting close.

WILD BOARS

Type	Location	HP
Passive/ Aggro	Woodlands, farmlands	20

Wild boars are skittish, and while they'll flee if they feel threatened, they also won't hesitate to attack. You can lure them to your side with meat or vegetables. If you choose to hunt them, they drop animal bones and meat.

WOLVES

Type	Location	HP
Aggro	Riverside, near water	350

Wolves are aggressive, and won't hesitate to attack you on sight if their pack spots you. If you hunt them, you can get animal bones and meat, but you can also tame them with meat. They generally spawn at night, but can still be found during the day if they survive the night.

THE 3 BASICS:
SURVIVING - WEAPONS

The final branch of mastering survival is weaponry, and understanding the vast and diverse arsenal that Fortnite has to offer. And we mean diverse. This is a game that enables you to land the final blow with anything from a pumpkin rocket launcher to a well-placed Loot Shark (trust me, it's happened, and it's really not a dignified way to go out).

So yeah, it's kind of unfair for anyone to be expected to know the ins-and-outs of every single weapon in-game, especially since the offering changes almost as often as players leap from the Battle Bus, with season theming, updates and of course, the vault. But with all of that going on, you really only need to step back and look at the bigger picture when it comes to weapons: ammo, rarity, upgrading, crafting and types.

WEAPON AMMO

Most weapons (excluding melee) in Fortnite require ammo, and each weapon type has a specific ammo requirement.

Ammo is a pretty easy find, as it spawns in chests, ammo boxes, supply drops and even just lying out there on the ground. Players can carry up to 999 of any type of ammo, so don't be stingy when it comes to picking it up - you're better with than without. The only exception to the 999 cap is rockets because of their brute power. Carrying 999 would be massively OP, so the max is capped at 12 in Battle Royale, and capped at 60 in Creative.

	Ammo Type	Weapon Type	Damage Per Shot	Effective Range
	Light Ammo	Pistols, SMGs	Low	Close
	Medium Ammo	Pistols, Assault Rifles	Medium	Mid
	Heavy Ammo	Sniper Rifles	High	Long
	Shells	Shotguns	High	Close
	Rockets	Explosives	Very High	Mid/Long

*There are other ammo types, like Arrows and Energy, but the corresponding weapons are often season-specific or vaulted.

WEAPON RARITY

Just like other items and cosmetics in Fortnite, weapons fall under the same six tiered rarity hierarchy. The rarity indicates both the weapon's power and your chances of finding it on the island.

The general rule when it comes to rarity is the higher the rarity, the better the weapon - but don't be mindless when it comes to following the colour system. Try to keep a balanced weapon selection as much as possible; there's no point in tossing a lower-rarity long range weapon to add yet another close range weapon to your collection just because it's a higher tier. Ultimately, weapon type and range is more important to consider than rarity, because who knows what kind of situation awaits you just around the corner. Be prepared, balance is key!

Common
Uncommon
Rare
Epic
Legendary
Mythic
Exotic

TIP:

Exotic weapons are the latest addition to Fortnite arsenal and are very rare - you can only get one by buying one from certain NPCs using Bars. For more information on NPCs, check out the Island Dwellers chapter on p. 46-47.

UPGRADING WEAPONS

A weapon's rarity isn't necessarily fixed, and there are ways of boosting your current arsenal's power without having to actually swap any guns out.

UPGRADE BENCHES

Upgrade Benches were first introduced back at the dawn of Chapter 2, and while they were vaulted in Season 5, they made their return in Chapter 7. These objects can be found across the island (mostly in POIs and key landmarks) and allow players to either upgrade a weapon. They require Bars to upgrade.

NPC SERVICES

It depends on your current season, but Characters can also offer upgrading services. They also take Bars as a form of payment, and can increase a weapon's rarity, stats and effectiveness. The higher the tier, the higher the cost in Bars. As we said before, this function depends on the season, as the devs seem to flip between having Characters offer upgrading or having Upgrade Benches on the map, so be sure to check your current patch notes to find out what method is available for you to boost your weaponry.

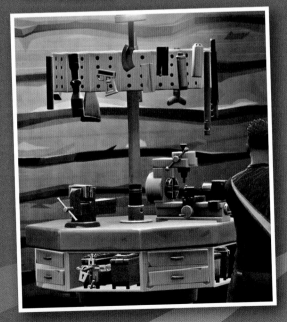

CRAFTING

Crafting is a new mechanic introduced in Chapter 2: Season 6, that allows players to gather components from around the island and use them to alter a weapon. While it began with Animal Bones and Stink Sacs, it has since evolved and become a more streamlined system.

> **TIP:**
>
> What's the difference between Crafting and Upgrading? Crafting is done entirely in the player inventory, and only requires materials - no Character or Bench needed.

So what do we need to start Crafting? Just some crafting ingredients, which are likely to be Nuts and Bolts. These can be found in red toolboxes scattered throughout the map, but you can also acquire some by breaking anything that looks vaguely mechanical with your pickaxe, like cars, TVs and even fire hydrants.

To pull up the Crafting menu, hit the Tab key and use the E key to cycle through. Choose the weapon you wish to Craft and you'll see its specs and the required ingredients. If you have the requirements, you can hit Craft and have that new weapon dropped right into your Inventory.

> **TIP:**
>
> The crafting process takes 3 seconds to complete, so it's not exactly the best pick to do mid-fight. Make sure you're alone and have decent cover before starting.

WEAPON TYPES

There are always wild new weapons being introduced in the world of Fortnite, but no matter how wacky they get, they usually all fall into the general weapon categories established since Day 1.

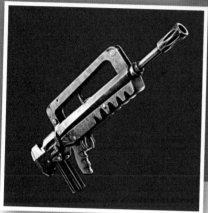

ASSAULT RIFLES

Assault Rifles are effective across medium to long ranges, and their high damage makes them some of the best balanced weapons available. They also have a medium to high capacity magazine, which means you can lay down some continuous fire on targets or structures.

- Assault Rifles unfortunately have pretty rough bloom, so fire in short bursts to take advantage of that first shot accuracy.

- Damage fall off for these guns begins at 50m, reaching a minimal damage value of 66% at 100m.

SNIPER RIFLES

Where an Assault Rifle can't, a Sniper Rifle can. These long range bad-boys deal a lot of damage from a distance, but their efficiency relies pretty heavily on a player's tracking ability and aim skills, as well as the bullet's travel speed.

- If you're aiming at a target in the distance that's moving, aim ahead of them to compensate for bullet speed and drop.

- Sniper rifles are great at long range, but their slow fire rate makes them useless in close quarters. Make sure you're ready to switch to another weapon if you are ambushed while sniping.

PISTOLS

Pistols are the middleman that do decently enough if you find one upon landing, but are never anyone's top pick for a loadout. Still, this basic gun is effective at close and mid-range and is a decent option when used in combination with a Rifle or SMG.

- Light Ammo pistols have excellent hip fire accuracy.

- Pistols have the widest range of variety within their category, so be sure to inspect your pick-up before you start shooting.

SMGS

Submachine Guns (SMGs) are best used at close range, as they have a high damage per second but high damage drop off and bullet spray. Up close, they're formidable, but anything from mid-range and back, they're about as impactful as a light summer breeze.

- Be sure to use controlled bursts when it comes to firing SMGs. Their high fire rate may be satisfying, but it's easy to lose count of how much ammo it's chomping through.

- SMGs are a good choice for weapon combos - use another gun to deal damage while closing the distance before finishing the opponent off with an SMG at close range.

SHOTGUNS

Shotguns are another close-range devastator, with a high DPS and area of effect. They're unbeatable up close, but the drop off is very real, as they often struggle to connect at even just mid-range. It may be useless at a distance, but it's worth it for the havoc it wreaks up close.

- The shotgun is a duellers gun, so equip one when you're building your 90s and taking on 1v1s.

- You can cheat the reload time a little by regularly topping up your ammo - partial reloads are faster than full reloads.

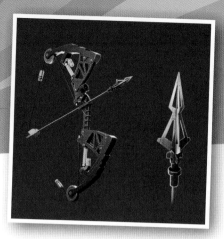

EXPLOSIVES

Explosive weapons are made for ranged combat, and are often better suited for shooting down structures and vehicles than smaller targets like players. Their huge damage comes at the cost of a slow fire rate, so if your target is moving, you'll need to predict their trajectory and aim ahead.

- Explosives have splash damage, so don't go whipping one out at close quarters unless you're willing to take some damage too.

- These are definitely the most effective weapons at destroying builds. One rocket to a foundation will bring it down in a flash.

CROSSBOWS/BOWS

Of all the weapon types, crossbows/bows probably spend the most time in the vault, but if you happen to be playing a season where there's a variant on the loose, then remember they're best for long-range combat. These are projectile weapons, which require the same predictive tracking as explosives.

- Don't even bother trying to use these against structures, as the damage they deal is pretty poor.

- Bows get targeting arcs, like using a throwable.

THROWABLES

These weapons usually come in the form of grenades, mines and bombs, but they often have utility purposes as well as damage.

WINNING THE 1V1:
PVP

The core element of any Battle Royale game lies in the most frantic experience it has to offer: the 1v1. You could be minding your own business and chasing after chickens or you could have seen that player coming from all the way across the map - there's no way to avoid it, and whether you're a hunter or a pacifist, you're going to have to engage in a 1v1 if you want to earn that Victory Royale.

There's no way to know for sure what your opponent is packing, but there's always ways to increase your chances of having the upper hand: by failing to prepare, you're preparing to fail.

LOADOUT

Your loadout is all you have to work with when it comes down to a 1v1, and you won't be able to really change things up or reconfigure in the middle of crossfire. Keeping on top of your loadout throughout the match is your most crucial form of preparation, and you want to make sure you're keeping it optimal: 2 Weapons - 2 Heals - 1 Dealer's Choice. Prioritize getting yourself an Assault Rifle, and make sure you have smaller healing items (Small Shield Potions/Bandages etc.) so you can heal quickly if you take fire mid-fight.

KEEP THEM GUESSING

Movement is just as key to your survivability as your aim, and when it comes to 1v1s, you've got to keep it random. You want to be as unpredictable as possible to throw off your enemy - if you continuously run from side to side, a savvy opponent will detect the pattern and aim ahead of you, catching you out. Keep it fresh: zig zag side to side, back to front, and make good use of cover. Jumping is a great way to throw off your movement pattern too, and allows you a brief opportunity to line-up a headshot on your descent.

ALTITUDE ADVANTAGE

It's an adage that applies to any shooter: the high ground advantage. It's easier to aim and shoot down than up. When traversing the map, try to stick to higher-altitude paths so you have a better lay of the land around you, and are in a prime position to shoot if need be. If you find yourself on the wrong end of a hill-side battle, don't hesitate to build yourself to more advantageous ground (be sure to practice the Go-to Builds in this guide's building chapter).

SHOOT - BUILD - REPOSITION

Forget eat - sleep - repeat; this is your new mantra to live by. Shoot - Build - Reposition should be on loop while heading into a duel: take your shots, build walls to eat damage and then reposition yourself to throw off enemy tracking before starting the circuit all over again. This is a foundational practice for 1v1s that obviously requires some adaptation per fight (like placing a pause in the Build to heal up, or foregoing the defensive if your enemy is floundering), but is key to know.

CHOOSE YOUR BATTLES

When the win condition of any Battle Royale game is to stay alive, the most effective tip for 1v1s is really knowing when to bow out, or avoid engagement. Not all fights go your way, but that doesn't mean that death is your only option. Likewise, it's not a game over if you spot an enemy in the distance and you're all out of ammo.

Keep a constant eye on your resources - they'll dictate whether the fight is worth the investment or not. If you see an enemy before they see you, take pause to take stock. Is your loadout ready for a duel? Are you in a good position to engage, or do you have to relocate? Do you have enough mats to see this through? Do you have enough HP/Shields right now, or enough items to recover if you take a hit? If the answer is no to any of these, sneak away and get yourself sorted before they spot you.

You want to be equally as aware of the tide of battle mid-fight, too. If the opponent is more robust than you thought, ask if it's worth burning through your resources for one elimination. Be aware of any exit routes you could take if things go south.

WINNING THE 1V1:
PVE

It's not just enough to know how to deal with other players anymore. With the introduction of AI in Chapter 2, the island has gone hostile, and you have to keep an eye out for game-spawned enemies just as much as fellow gamers.

WILDLIFE

When it comes to taking on some of Fortnite's more formidable forms of wildlife, it's important to measure the risk just as much as you would taking on a player. Boars are the easiest of the aggro animals to take out due to their size. When it comes to wolves, they often move in packs, so don't let them spot you if you're low on HP. If Raptors are roaming the island in your current season, be ready to toss some meat to distract them if you need to make an escape.

TIP:
For more information on wildlife, check out the Wildlife chapter on p. 18-19

HENCHMEN

Henchmen patrol certain POIs across the island. If they spot you, a question mark will appear above their heads, and if they're ready to fight, it will change to an exclamation.

Treat a Henchmen duel the same as you would a non-threatening PvP duel; their AI isn't super sophisticated and their HP isn't too high, so they're not super dangerous, but they can cause some inconvenient damage if you don't deal with them efficiently. Random movement works really well against them as the AI's tracking isn't great at predicting. Jump up and take the headshot if you can.

Once you down a henchman, you can shake them down to gain intel on the surrounding area, giving locations for chests, other henchmen and bosses.

TIP:
For more information on friendly and hostile NPCs, check out the Island Dwellers chapter on p.46-47

BOSSES

Bosses are hostile Characters that pose more of a threat: they've got more HP, they've got more Shields, and they have a lot more to offer (in the form of Exotic or Mythic gear) should you take them down. They're a tougher opponent than any wildlife or Henchman, so keep these tips in mind when taking them on.

TIP:
Don't forget that the Boss line-up changes per season, so take a look online to check your current season locations if you're struggling to find them ingame.

- Keep your distance. If you can, try to open the fight with high-ground and a headshot before they actively engage. Most Bosses have 400 Shield and 100 Health, so a couple of well-placed headshots with a powerful Sniper Rifle can really tip the tide in your favour early.

- If you're playing in a season with Henchmen, deal with them first. Taking on a Boss while there are groups of Henchmen still around is dangerous, as they will contribute to the Boss' assault.

- Skilled players can use the storm to their advantage when taking on bosses - get the timing just right and you can count on the Boss falling into the purple to hasten their downfall alongside your assault.

- Stay vigilant! Bosses only spawn once per match, so there's a good chance you're not the only player trying to seek them out and take them down. Keep an eye out during the fight for other players who might take the opportunity to snipe out two enemies while they're otherwise distracted.

FISHING 101

Fishing splashed onto the scene with the arrival of Chapter 2, and has evolved considerably since its introduction. Do you remember back when there were only three types of fish you could catch? Ha. The good old days.

Now fishing has become its own kind of mini-game, with more varieties of fish to catch, more weapons to unearth, and most importantly, more reasons to actually consider kicking back and casting a line when there are 99 people out there actively trying to kill you.

THE ESSENTIALS

Firstly, you've got to find the perfect fishing spot. You can fish in active Fishing Spots (marked by the bubbling white circle on the water's surface) or in calm waters. Fishing Spots yield better fish and better loot, so try to seek them out if you've got the chance. Next, you've got to choose your tool:

- **Fishing Rod (Common):** These spawn across the map in barrels and on the ground. You'll likely find them nearby any prime angling spots.

- **Pro Fishing Rod (Rare):** These have a higher chance of pulling rarer fish and loot. They can be found in barrels and on the ground, or upgraded from a regular Fishing Rod.

- **Harpoon Gun (Rare):** This short-range weapon can be used for high-speed fishing, but can only be used in active Fishing Spots.

- **Explosives:** When all else fails, go in with a bang. Shooting a Fishing Spot with a rocket gives a super quick payout.

CATCH OF THE SEASON

So who exactly are the deepsea denizens of the island's waters? There's plenty to come across, with different types giving different gameplay benefits, like shields and health. Here are the nine categories of fish you can catch:

FLOPPERS

Floppers are Uncommon fish that can be found pretty much anywhere. They have a carry limit of 4, and a size range of 30-60 cm. They heal 40 HP (up to 100 HP).

Flopper Type	Orange Flopper	Green Flopper	Blue Flopper
Location	Anywhere	Anywhere	Anywhere

SLURPFISH

Slurpfish are an Epic catch that are more commonly found in Fishing Spots than calm waters. They have a carry limit of 3, and a size range of 30-60 cm. They heal 40 HP/Shield.

Slurpfish Type	Blue Slurpfish	Yellow Slurpfish	Purple Slurpfish	Black Slurpfish	White Slurpfish
Location	Anywhere	Swamps	Mountains	Coastal (at night)	Swamps (at night, with Pro Fishing Rod)

JELLYFISH

Jellyfish are Rare, and can be used to heal several players. They have a carry limit of 3, and heal 20 HP/Shield to the player that consumes it and surrounding players.

Jellyfish Type	Slurp Jellyfish	Dark Vanguard Jellyfish	Cuddle Jellyfish	Peely Jellyfish	Purple Jellyfish
Location	Anywhere	Swamps (at night)	Anywhere	Mountains (with Pro Fishing Rod)	Coastal

SHIELD FISH

Shield Fish are Rare, with a carry limit of 3, and a size range of 35-65 cm. They heal 50 Shield.

Shield Fish Type	Black and Blue Shield Fish	Black Striped Shield Fish	Pink Shield Fish	Green Shield Fish	Light Blue Shield Fish
Location	Anywhere	Coastal	Anywhere (with Pro Fishing Rod)	Forests	Anywhere

SPICY FISH

Spicy Fish are Rare catches, with a carry limit of 3, and a size range of 30-60 cm. They can heal 15 HP, and give the user a speed boost for 1 minute.

Spicy Fish Type	Molten Spicy Fish	Drift Spicy Fish	White Spotted Spicy Fish	Southern Spicy Fish	Sky Blue Spicy Fish
Location	Anywhere	Forests	Mountains	Swamps	Coastal

SMALL FRY

Small Fry are Common fish, with a carry limit of 6, and a size range of just 15-25 cm. They heal 25 HP (up to 75 HP).

Small Fry Type	Light Blue Small Fry	Tan Small Fry	Purple Top Small Fry	Black Small Fry	Blue Small Fry
Location	Anywhere	Anywhere	Anywhere	Anywhere (at night)	Coastal

HOP FLOPPERS

Hop Floppers are an Epic catch, with a carry limit of 3, and a huge size range of 5-100 cm. They heal 25 HP (up to 75 HP).

Hop Flopper Type	Drift Hop Flopper	Coho Hop Flopper	Atlantic Hop Flopper	Chinhook Hop Flopper	Chum Hop Flopper
Location	Anywhere	Forests	Mountains (with Pro Fishing Rod)	Swamps	Coastal

STINK FLOPPERS

Stink Floppers are an Uncommon fish, with a carry limit of 3, and a size range of 35-70 cm. They heal 20 HP, and can also be used as a projectile weapon, creating a cloud of toxic gas that deals 5 damage per tick.

Stink Flopper Type	Blue Stink Flopper	Clown Stink Flopper	Purple Stink Flopper
Location	Anywhere	Anywhere	Anywhere

CUDDLE FISH

Cuddle Fish are Rare fish, with a carry limit of 6, and a huge size range of 35-70 cm. They deal 35 HP worth of damage to any enemy they can attach themselves to.

Cuddle Fish Type	Cuddle Fish	Blue Cuddle Fish	Green Cuddle Fish	Orange Cuddle Fish	Red Cuddle Fish
Location	Anywhere	Anywhere	Anywhere	Anywhere	Anywhere

There are also super rare fish like the fabled Mythic Goldish, that can deal an insta-kill if thrown. The game regularly debuts and vaults super rare and powerful fish (the Vendetta Flopper, Zero Point Fish and Rift Fish to name a few).

TIP:

When thrown, a fish can act like a beacon by pinging its location to your squadmates once it has landed.

SNOWY FLOPPER

THERMAL FISH

KEEPING UP WITH THE COLLECTION:

You can keep up to date with your fishing feats in the Fishing Collection Book. This book shows you all the fish you've managed to collect throughout the season, including the amount you've caught, and your personal best length compared to your friends'.

OTHER CATCHES

There's more than just fish lurking beneath the surface, you know. You can also catch a bunch of weapons, from Assault Rifles and Pistols to Sniper Rifles and of course, the trusty old Rusty Can. Just like the fish, you've got a better chance of finding rarer weapons in Fishing Spots than in calm waters.

PICK YOUR PLAYSTYLE

For the most part, Fortnite's a game of luck and chance (like finding Shield potions at your landing spot or, you know, not accidentally stumbling into a Raptor nest), but there's one constant: how you choose to play.

There's no one set way to win at Battle Royale. Everyone has their preferences as to how they want to tackle the task at hand when they drop in to the map, and as Fortnite has evolved from its 2017 debut, there are more and more options to consider. So whether you're ready to rush in guns-a-blazin', hang back and heal, build an impenetrable fortress or magically convert yourself into a Slurp barrel to avoid an enemy, there's room for you in Fortnite.

THE CLASSIC

The Classic playstyle is a true Jack-of-All-Trades - where a player will draw from all of the game's mechanics without focusing or specializing on anything specific. Think of this as the standard Fortnite experience: putting together a balanced loadout, and taking on gunfights and building structures when necessary.

This playstyle is well suited for both new players who are getting used to what Fortnite has to offer, as well as seasoned players who just prefer a more casual experience when playing. Classic never goes out of style, so it's a good option to default to at the start of a new season while you feel out what's new.

THE HUNTER

The Hunter drops from the Battle Bus, picks up a gun and is ready to rack up that kill count. They work with a weapon-weighted loadout, make use of stealth options to catch you off-guard, no-scope like it's no sweat and almost always have the high ground advantage. The new Bounty system plays right into this style, rewarding players for actively hunting others down.

This playstyle is best suited to players coming from more FPS-heavy games that are familiar with gunplay mechanics. Comparatively, it has a really high skill-ceiling and requires a lot of practice to execute efficiently - it's best for those comfortable with the map and particularly weapons and their potential combos.

THE MEDIC

This playstyle is only available in duo/ team gameplay, as it ultimately leaves the gun-toting conflict to a teammate while you play a supportive role from a safe distance. You can keep a loadout weighted towards healing items while wielding weapons like Bandage Bazookas and Chug Cannons - and if those are vaulted, you can always chuck a Jellyfish or two for splash healing.

The Medic style is best suited for players who enjoy playing with teammates, but don't love engaging in duels unless absolutely necessary. It's good for those who prefer to contribute in a supportive way.

THE ARCHITECT

Fortnite's building mechanics are truly unique in the Battle Royale genre, and Architects take full advantage of everything the system has to offer. While they can hold their own in a fight, their true prowess lies in their mats, and they're able to force a battle into the skies with a tower or build a bridge right out of conflict in the blink of an eye.

The Architect style is another playstyle with a high skill-ceiling, as those who truly excel with it are masters at building. The best way to improve is to hone your skills in Creative and the Battle Lab until you're throwing up forts with muscle memory.

THE PACIFIST

Sometimes it's fun to see how far you can get without actively going aggro. Pacifists take the softer approach, prioritising outrunning the storm, keeping an ear out for gunshots in the distance to avoid and ready to escape and heal should they be ambushed. It's perfectly plausible to play it safe right into the top 10, and take out the last players within the final bubble.

The Pacifist style is best for those who want to explore the island more and try the game's other mechanics out like fishing and Character encounters.

PRO SURVIVAL TIPS

So you've covered the basics of gathering, building and surviving, learned all about dueling PvP and PvE, gone into the depths of the fishing mechanic and analysed the different playstyles you may come across on the island... What's left? Well, you've pretty much got it all, but there are some specific tips to surviving that don't quite fit into the previous nine chapters (wild, I know), so let's get them out of the way before we board that Battle Bus.

PLAY BY THE STORM

- It's easy to forget that with 99 other players, henchmen, bosses, and even wildlife out there trying to get you, that there's one unrelenting force out there that you just can't beat: the storm. Every strategic decision you make should be made with the storm firmly in mind.

- Try to stay close to the storm's edge when the eye shrinks, as most players tend to run as close to the middle of the eye as they can. You can also hang out near the edges and snipe out any incoming players trying to run to safety.

- If you play it smart, you can use the storm to help you against some of the game's bosses. Tougher bosses to take down aren't immune to the storm, and don't have the Ai to continually heal up and make the reparations that you do when in the purple.

KEEP IT CAUTIOUS

- If there's a huge pile of very enticing, clearly kill-drop loot left on the ground, then pause - it might be a trap. Check there aren't any lingering players waiting to lure you in unsuspectedly before you dive in and start working out whether you need to swap any loot in or out.

- Also, if you've just won a 1v1, don't wipe your bow just yet. There's a good chance it may have drawn some attention, so quickly scout the immediate area before sifting through loot or doing any long loading healing. If you're late game, you may want to build around yourself while looting, just to be safe.

COVER YOUR TRACKS

- Be sure to close doors behind you when you enter buildings - an open door is a surefire sign someone's been in there, and might invite other players to try to sneak up on you mid-looting. It also acts as somewhat of an alarm system for you, because you'll be able to hear the door open if someone follows you in.

- When you're harvesting from trees, try to stop before the final blow. This will prevent the tree from disappearing from the map in a big swoosh animation, alerting far-off foes to your location.

- A really basic but fundamental tip is to keep the noise to an absolute minimum. Walk or crouch when you know you've got company to get the spring on your enemy (you can toggle default running in the settings), and don't go hacking cars for the sake of it to set alarms off.

- Even switching and reloading weapons makes a detectable audio cue, and they're specific to each weapon type. If you play long enough, it may be able to give you a clue as to what your unsuspecting enemy is packing, but remember - your opponent can make the same read.

- You might be able to hide your character, but you can't mask their footsteps. Be sure to listen out for any footsteps to work out where your enemy is.

THE SOUND OF VICTORY

- You'd be surprised how big of a role sound plays in the whole equation. If you can, opt to play with headphones instead of speakers. You can hear so much more subtle sounds with headphones that can mean the difference between life and death.

THE ISLAND:
WELCOME TO APOLLO

This is where the magic happens, folks: the Island, AKA Code Name: Apollo, AKA the map. You better get used to this expanse of land, kids, because this is where every single match is going to take place - it's the backdrop for Battle Royale, and what kind of victor doesn't know his arena inside and out?

When Chapter 2 came with a brand new island, players had a lot to discover and re-learn. But we're deep into the Apollo era now - this new island is just as familiar a friend as the previous one, and it keeps it on our toes just as much, too, with new features, POIs and even dwellers with each update.

CENTRAL ACTIVITY

Apollo Island has the distinction of changing the center of the map to fit the season's theme. From the Authority overtaking the Agency, to the Spire exploding and leaving behind the extra-terrestrial Aftermath, the center of the map has seen a lot of changes. As a result, the center of the map has become key in the game's story telling, and often is a required visit for a lot of the seasonal challenges.

WAS THAT ALWAYS THERE?

Be sure to keep an eye out when traversing the map, because the developers really like to hide little easter eggs throughout the island hinting at the next big update.

TEMPORARY TENANTS

This island seems to see a lot more changes than the original map, as locations regularly pop in and out with different updates. Sometimes you can even visit locations based on their collaborations, like Stark Industries rifting on top of Frenzy Farm and the Orchard in Chapter 2: Season 4, before disappearing in Season 5.

YOU'RE NOT ALONE

It used to just be another 99 players you had to look out for, but with new additions, the island is truly thriving with different forms of life - some of which want to end yours. For more information, check out the Wildlife chapter on p. 18-19 and the Island Dwellers chapter on p. 46-47.

NAILING THE LANDING

Battle Royale is all about survival, and that starts as soon as you leap out of that Battle Bus. Don't underestimate how important your landing spot is: it's surprisingly key to your potential victory, because the first moments are always crucial.

HOW TO LAND

2. **Aim high.** Yep. Switch it up as soon as the glider is in play, because as soon as that sucker pops out, you want to start looking for some verticality to get up on. This gives you the immediate high ground advantage if there are others in the area, and gives you a bit more time to get the lay of the land. Even if there aren't any towers or anything where you fall, just remember: it's always better to land on a roof as opposed to the middle of the street.

There's a lot of variety in Fortnite but landing might just be the one thing where there's one, inarguably superior way to make your way from the Battle Bus down to the island.

1. **Go low.** There's two stages to every descent: the skydive and the glide. Skydiving is way faster than gliding, but the glider will auto-deploy as soon as you reach a certain distance from the ground. That means if you aim for lower ground, you'll maximize your dive time and landing speed. But that's only half of it, because when you're done going low, then you've got to...

40

WHERE TO LAND

So where's the best place to land? Well, there's no one spot... But there are a bunch of tips you should keep in mind before you tip the driver and go geronimo.

1. Know your seasonal Hot Drops. A Hot Drop is a popular spot for players to land, and are usually POIs that lie along the Battle Bus route. While they're definitely loot heavy, there's also going to be a lot more competition, with early skirmishes practically guaranteed. If you're playing for a kill count, then go ahead, but if you're looking to play a more strategic game, best to avoid them.

2. But sometimes... Sometimes you've just got to charge right in with the rush, right? Hot Drops are Hot for a reason, you know. If you do find yourself headed for a Hot Spot, at least keep an exit strategy in mind as you maneuver through the chaos. Get in, get what you need, and get out.

3. If you're not so keen on the guaranteed madness of a Hot Spot, be sure then be sure not to skew too far in the opposite direction. If you land too remotely, you may struggle to put together your loadout and gather your mats. You want to be ready to go ASAP, and that can be hard if you land on top of a mountain with nothing but snow and the odd tent.

4. Remember - landing is a balance between safety and resources. For Hot Drops, you sacrifice safety for a plethora of resources, but landing in the deserted shack in the bottom corner sacrifices resources for safety. Try to get some distance from the Battle Bus route, but stick to POIs and Landmarks.

HIT THE GROUND RUNNING

As soon as you've secured the landing, it's time to secure the bag, and by bag, I mean loadout. The race starts as soon as you touch the ground, so get ready to start swinging your Pickaxe for mats, glugging down Shield Potions ASAP and prioritize finding a weapon: if you're in a Hot Spot, a close-range gun like a Shotgun is ideal to deal with nearby players, but if you're somewhere less popping, wait until you find a mid/long range gun before you take off.

GETTING AROUND THE MAP

So you've landed in your prime spot, gathered some mats, grabbed some loot and are feeling pretty good about your loadout - it's time to get exploring the island. Whether you're one to avoid crowds or actively seek out those headshots, there's one element of gameplay that remains the same: you're always on the move. There's a lot of ground to cover across this island, and hey, good news - you don't have to do it all on foot.

BY LAND

A big addition to transport came in Chapter 2: Season 3, with the addition of cars. There are four types you can take for a joyride, but remember - just like real cars, these all require fuel to drive. You can refuel cars at gas stations, or by using gas cans found across the map.

OG BEAR

- Seats: 2
- HP: 1,200
- Fuel Capacity: 150

The OG Bear is a pickup truck, and has the distinction of being the only car that maintains its speed both on and off road. It can also float in water too, should you find yourself making a desperate swerve. They spawn with anywhere between 50 and 150 fuel.

ISLANDER PREVALENT

- Seats: 4
- HP: 800
- Fuel Capacity: 100

The Prevalent is a sedan-type car that is the most common discovery across the island (hence the name). There are three types: a Prevalent, a Prevalent GG2020 and a taxi. They spawn with anywhere between 40 and 100 fuel.

TITANO MUDFLAP

- Seats: 2
- HP: 1,200
- Fuel Capacity: 150

This semi-truck is a juggernaut, and works just as well as a battering ram for ploughing into player builds and obstacles than it does for getting from A to B. These spawn with 80-100 fuel.

VICTORY MOTORS WHIPLASH

- Seats: 2
- HP: 800
- Fuel Capacity: 100

The Whiplash is a flashier ride than the Prevalent, with a kind of supercar-esque sleekness to it. It has a boost function that allows extra speed at the cost of more fuel. Like the Prevalent, it spawns with 40-100 fuel.

TIP:

Cars have a radio feature, so you can listen to different radio stations while cruising the island. You can listen to Fortnite's soundtrack, as well as licensed music from artists like Drake, the Weekend, BTS and even Eiffel 65 for that throwback.

BY WATER

Water became a huge part of the new map when Chapter 2 first launched, so it only makes sense that they also introduced a new vehicle for you to cross it with. With Patch 15.10, Motorboats now run on fuel, too, and can be refuelled with gas cans. Ran out of fuel? No worries - you can always hitch a ride on a shark. Yep, you read that right.

MOTORBOAT

- Seats: 4
- HP: 800

Motorboats come equipped with single-shot missiles that can deal 35 damage. They also have a boost function that gains a lot of speed on water. Interestingly, motorboats can also travel on land, but they lose 1 HP of health per second when travelling, and 2 HP per second when boosting.

LOOT SHARK

If you've got a Fishing Rod, then you can ride a Loot Shark like a jetski. Of course, this is a way rarer form of travel than the other methods - don't be outrunning the storm and be waiting at the docks for a shark to get you out of there. But it's a fun little Easter Egg if it presents itself, and always makes for a good screenshot or two.

BY AIR

Sometimes it's best to take to the skies, whether it's just a touch above you or all the way up in the skybox.

ZIPLINE

Ziplines debuted back in the very first Season 7, and give you a speedy mobility boost. What makes them super useful is that you can still use your weapons and items while zipping from Point A to Point B, but they also make you somewhat of a sitting duck, so be ready to make a quick drop off to disrupt your trajectory if someone spots you.

TIP:

Hitscan weapons are the best to use on a zipline, as they're easiest to use when moving.

LAUNCH PAD/GLIDER

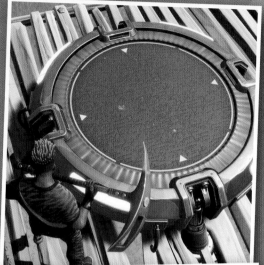

This method is sometimes the quickest way to get out of harm's way - throwing down a quick Launch Pad and using your Glider to sail on out of there. It's a great way to cover distance if you find yourself stuck in the storm, and the higher the launch point, the better.

TIP:

Remember that Launch Pads can be used by anyone on the map, which makes them a precarious choice if you're using one mid-duel for an exit strategy. The enemy you were trying to escape might just follow your tail and be gliding down behind you, so keep your guard up when using one.

'TIS THE SEASON

Like weapons, the Fortnite vehicle roster is always changing depending on the season. Driftboards and Shopping Carts to B.R.U.T.E. mechs and flying saucers, there's always a new and different way to make your way across the island. Be sure to check out the patch notes for your current season so you're not caught unawares if you stumble across a Choppa, or spot another player being launched out of a pirate cannon.

TIP:

Don't forget that you can participate in Quadcrasher races in Party Royale. Just look for the Quadcrasher Motocross in coordinate C5.

ISLAND DWELLERS

QUESTS LEAVING SOON   ISABELLE   CREATIVE SHOWCASE

ISABELLE

An adept student of the arcane arts by day, and an enchanted explorer by night.

You're not alone - and it's not just other players shooting at your heels now. The Fortnite island is more alive than ever, teeming with all sorts of life, from wild to... well, humans. The game first kinda dabbled with the idea of in-world characters throughout its loosely-told storyline, but Chapter 2 Season 5 brought us one of the biggest changes Fortnite has seen since its debut, with the addition of NPCs (non-playable characters) dotted across the island for you to interact with.

FINDING A FRIEND

TIP:

You'll know you're close to an NPC when a speech bubble icon appears on your map.

NPCs can be encountered all across the map, but their location generally changes season by season. Check online for the latest location updates for your current season if you're having trouble tracking them down! Also remember that NPCs spawn once per match - if another player has gotten to them first and hired them or taken them out, then they're gone for that round.

You and I have so much in common! Human skin, human face, human emotions, etcetera!

TIP:

Spitting Bars are a special type of in-match currency that can be used to purchase items or services from NPCs. You can earn Bars by eliminating opponents, opening safes, completing bounties, and destroying items like cash registers, sofas, and beds.

If you do manage to reach an NPC first, you will have the chance to interact with them. What they can do/offer you depends on the Season you're currently playing, as the developers regularly mix up NPC interactions with each update.

Bounty	Duel	Hire	Locate	Quest	Upgrade Weapon
Place a bounty on a nearby player.	Fight the character to win a weapon.	Recruit the character to fight alongside you.	Locate an item for the character.	Receive a quest from the character to earn Bars.	Upgrade your current weapon.

FIGHTING A FOE

But not all NPCs are there to make nice. This is Battle Royale, of course, so there are a fair few (well, more than a fair few, to be honest) NPCs that are out for blood.

- Henchmen were introduced in Chapter 2, Season 2. They generally vary in theming and appearance every by season, but they have a few constants: all of them are packing heat (from Heavy Assault Rifles to Suppressed Sniper Rifles), they have around 100 health and they can be shaken down for Scanners.

- Bosses are the toughest NPCs to take down. They have much more HP and Shields than Henchmen, and can drop Mythic, Legendary, Epic or Rare gear if you manage to take them out. Bosses differ visually from Henchmen too, as they all wear ingame skins the player can also unlock.

 TIP:

For more information on duelling NPCs, check out Winning the 1v1: PvE on p. 28-29!

CHARACTER COLLECTION BOOK

The Character Collection Book is a lobby feature introduced in Chapter 2 Season 5 that allows you to keep track of the NPCs you've come across so far.

MAKING PROGRESS

Would it be shocking to hear that there's more to Fortnite than a Victory Royale? If being the last one standing was the only win the game offered, it would have fallen to the wayside among the other forgotten Battle Royales years ago. Fortnite provides a boatload of other achievements for the player to earn, with new systems to mark their progress across the game.

THE BATTLE PASS

The Battle Pass is an in-game progression system that rewards players for playing the game and levelling up. It changes each season, and has a really diverse range of prizes, from skins and emotes to gliders and pickaxes. The full Battle Pass requires V-Bucks to purchase, but there are still free rewards available for players who don't want to open their virtual wallets. Since its debut, there's been two methods of progression through the Pass:

1. Linear: This is the most prevalent throughout the seasons, and is pretty simple. When you play the game, you earn XP and make your way through the Pass, earning rewards as you level up and hit certain milestones. Think of this as the classic Battle Pass mode.

2. Battle Stars: This method first made an appearance in Chapter 1 before it was shelved, but it made a return in Chapter 2: Season 7. Battle Stars act as a kind of Battle Pass currency, allowing you to pick and choose the rewards you want that are on offer. It's not quite a free-for-all because some cosmetics do require all of the rewards on the page to be purchased to unlock, but you do have a lot more freedom on how to reap your rewards.

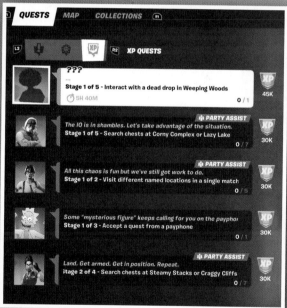

XP

Regardless of whether your current season is using the Classic Battle Pass or the Battle Stars system, what's universal is the need for XP.

XP is earned by simply playing matches and performing certain actions (like eliminating opponents), but can also be earned (and is more efficiently farmed) by completing challenges and quests.

BOOSTING YOUR XP TIPS:

Weekly Epic Quests: Epic releases seven Epic Quests for players to take on every week. If you make your way through them all, you can earn around 20,000 - 30,000 XP (depending on the season). The challenges usually reset on Thursdays, so be sure to get as many done as you can before they renew.

Weekly Legendary Quests: Legendary Quests are a tougher ask as they're more time-consuming, but they also promise 30,000 - 45,000 XP for each one. Sure, it's an effort, but the XP glean is definitely worth it.

Sharing is Caring: Playing with friends using the Party Assist function means any progress towards Epic and Legendary quests will be shared between everyone. This is perfect for the more laborious Legendary quests; 25 headshots go twice as fast with two people aiming.

Keep Up Your APM: Keep your digits active while you're playing a match, even if you're in a lull. You can earn XP from a bunch of inane in-game actions like destroying shrubs and thanking the bus drivers. Get the most out of each match by keeping busy.

HOW LONG WILL YOU SURVIVE?

You made it. You're here. 50 pages in and you've covered everything from where to land, where to aim, where to cast your line and where to get your Battle Pass filled. We've bestowed all of our wisest words upon you, so you should be ready to reign a bloody hellfire upon the island and all those poor fools unfortunate enough to be upon it when you touch down... If you've been paying attention, that is... Take this quiz and check your answers on p. 62-63 to see how long you'll survive.

1. What's the best balanced loadout option?

a. 2 Weapons - 2 Heals - 1 Dealer's Choice

b. 1 Weapon - 3 Heals - 1 Dealer's Choice

c. 3 Weapons - 1 Heal - 1 Dealer's Choice

d. 2 Weapons - 2 Heals - 2 Dealer's Choice

2. Oh no! You've found yourself in a duel you aren't prepared for - how do you proceed to escape?

a. Building 90s upwards

b. Building a ramp to highground

c. Ramp rushing to highground

d. Building turtles upwards

3. What type of ammo is best for long-range weaponry?

a. Light Ammo

b. Medium Ammo

c. Heavy Ammo

d. Shells

7. Which mat structure has the highest maximum HP?

a. Wood ramp

b. Stone floor

c. Metal wall

d. Metal roof

4. You're caught in the storm and all you've got in your loadout is a bunch of fish! What do you gobble down to keep you alive as you run to the eye?

a. Spicy Fish

b. Floppers

c. Shield Fish

d. Small Fry

8. You've taken damage mid-fight - what's the best method to heal up?

a. Medkit

b. Small Shield Potion

c. Bandage

d. Apple

5. What should you be thinking when you land?

a. Go low, aim high

b. Go low, aim low

c. Go high, aim low

d. Go high, aim high

9. You're riding a zipline and you've spotted an enemy - what's the best weapon to whip out?

a. Hitscan

b. Projectile

c. Throwable

d. Melee

6. What's the best weapon combo to close the distance and finish an opponent up close?

a. Sniper rifle + Shotgun

b. Pistol + Shotgun

c. SMG + Shotgun

d. Assault rifle + Shotgun

10. What's the 1v1 Duel mantra?

a. Shoot - Reposition - Build

b. Shoot - Build - Reposition

c. Build - Reposition - Shoot

d. Shoot - Build - Shoot

A FRIEND LIKE FORTNITE

 Fortnite has always had an enviably diverse list of friends they've collaborated with since debut: from John Wick to Jordans, Major Lazer to Marshmello, Punk'd to Pixar and Star Wars to Stranger Things. There's no world that doesn't fit into the weird and wonderful world of Fortnite.

This year marked another hallmark year for their collaboration flex list, with some of the biggest names in pop culture making their appearances on the island. Were you lucky enough to catch any of these crossovers live?

COMIC BOOK CROSSOVERS

FORTNITE X DC

DC Comics have been all over the island this year, with skins from classic characters like Batman, Superman, Harley Quinn, Catwoman and Deathstroke. There have also been appearances from other DC characters like the Green Arrow, and Teen Titans' Beast Boy and Raven.

BATMAN

HARLEY QUINN

FORTNITE X MARVEL

While DC may be the choice this year, Epic doesn't pick sides, as they've still kept their partnership with Marvel alive. It began with the legendary Avengers crossover back in 2018, and has been going strong since. 2021 saw the arrival of Ant Man (along with a little Ant Manor west of Holly Hedges).

FORTNITE X HORIZON

But the video game collabs didn't stop at just cosmetics. 2021 gave us the console-exclusive Aloy Cup, a duos tournament featuring Aloy herself, with a Horizon Zero Dawn bundle as the grand prize. The bundle featured Aloy's Spear Pickaxe, Blaze Canister Back Bling and Glinthawk Glider, alongside other Hero Zero Dawn themed goodies.

FORTNITE X ROCKET LEAGUE

Spring 2021 saw the return of the Rocket League Llama-Rama to send off Season 2 of Rocket League. The event ran for just over a week, culminating in a Party Royale concert by DJ and producer Kaskade, with an exclusive glimpse at the upcoming Season 3.

HITTING THE ARCADE

FORTNITE X STREET FIGHTER

Fortnite's foray into other video game franchises was strictly legends only, so it made perfect sense that Chun Li and Ryu made their way into the game in an item shop bundle back in February. The Street Fighter bundle included skins, as well as a training bag and emotes of their iconic Shoryuken and Lightning Kick moves as emotes.

FORTNITE X TOMB RAIDER

Oh, and who could forget the inclusion of the icon herself, Lara Croft? The worlds of Fortnite and Tomb Raider collided with the Mystery at Croft Manor experience, a Creative event set in Lara's iconic mansion. Lara herself became the first Video Game Legend to spawn on the map as a character AI, and could be found at the Stealthy Stronghold. She also featured in the Character Collection Book.

CHUN-LI & RYU

JOIN THE HUNT

FORTNITE

PREDATOR

BATTLE PASS EXCLUSIVE

JOIN THE HUNT

FORTNITE GOES TO HOLLYWOOD

FORTNITE X TERMINATOR

Fortnite delved into sci-fi cinema legends this year, starting in January with the debut of the Future War bundle. This bundle featured skins of the iconic Sarah Connor and, of course, the T-800, with a Techno-Grip Axe and a special Cyberdyne Salute emote.

FORTNITE X PREDATOR

January also saw the first appearance of the iconic Predator. Other than the Legendary skin, he also appeared as a hostile AI boss at the Stealthy Stronghold. Players who defeated him could acquire the Predator's Cloaking Device.

FORTNITE X ALIEN

It makes sense that Ridley Scott's Alien series followed the Predator collab, with the monstrous Xenomorph available as a skin purchase in February alongside one of sci-fi's most celebrated action heroes, Ellen Ripley. The Space Gear bundle also included an adorable Weyland-Yutani Cat Carrier, and of course, an emote reenacting the series' infamous chest-bursting scene.

FORTNITE X TRON: LEGACY

We also got a cosmetic crossover with the TRON: Legacy series, with an End of Line set featuring ten new futuristic and technological skins based on the Disney franchise hitting the ingame store. The crossover also saw a brand new glider modeled after the neon bikes used throughout the virtual reality series, and a backpack based on the franchise's combat discs.

THE BEAUTIFUL GAME

FORTNITE X NBA

Fortnite has been no stranger to dabbling in the sports realm before, with previous collabs including the NFL. This year saw Fortnite team up with the NBA in the Crossover, an event that brought Community Battles back to the game in May. There was also an NBA-themed Creative hub, as well as a ton of new NBA skins instore for fans to rep their favourite teams (and dunk some new Hookshot and Dribblin' emotes on that Victory Royale).

FORTNITE X FOOTBALL

The year kicked off with the Kickoff Set, giving players an opportunity to wear the uniform of their favourite football team. Fortnite collaborated with 23 clubs from all around the world, including Manchester City, Juventus, AC Milan and the Western Sydney Wanderers, to name a few. The cosmetics came alongside the Pelé Cup, as well as Pelé's iconic celebration move with the Pelé's Air Punch emote.

FORTNITE X NEYMAR JR.

Footballing legend Neymar Jr. was immortalized in the Fortnite Icon Series this year, and marked the first time a sports-themed outfit was based on a real life athlete. The Exhibition Style cosmetics featured the colours of the Brazilian flag, while the Primal Style cosmetics featured the colours of the French flag.

PRACTICE MAKES PERFECT:
CREATIVE + BATTLE LAB

| JULY CREW PACK | NEW LEGENDARY QUESTS | SEASON 7 BATTLE PASS | CREATIVE SHOWCASE |

TROPICAL THUNDER
Battle with your team for control of sky-high objectives in this community made LTM created by VYSENA!

As you've just learned for the past fifty or so pages, there's a whole lot of information to digest when it comes to mastering the art of the Victory Royale. Luckily, no one's expecting you to start making color-coded notes to study meticulously every night before you go to sleep - there are two in-game arenas that are perfect for you to drop into and practice your craft, or even blow off some steam.

CREATIVE

The Creative game mode is a place where players can build and share their own unique islands via the Creative hub. The sky's the limit here - you've got full access to the Fortnite asset library and you can use it to create whatever your heart desires, whether it's a classic sniper v. sniper showdown mode or a Super Mario deathrun (Google the code; you won't be disappointed).

But Creative isn't just a great place to play whacky game modes - there are also a lot of islands specifically crafted to help you practice certain gameplay elements, kind of like user-created training courses. There's a whole range out there, from aim training facilities and build war practices to quick warm-up courses to be run just before you jump off the Battle Bus.

MY ISLAND:
You hold all the power in the island in your little AR phone, your access to carefully placing a single banana on the ground or sending an Arctic Test Lab into the stratosphere. Don't worry; If you're not looking to build anything from scratch, you can also use ready-made prefabs (existing Fortnite assets) to populate your island.

FEATURED ISLANDS:
Featured Islands are a great way to try new game modes, as they have been created by other users and selected by Epic to showcase the best the community has to offer. If you want the chance to see your own island featured, you can submit it to the official Epic Games site.

TIP:

Each island has a unique 12-digit string code that identifies it. If you want to share your island with friends, or you're looking for a specific game mode you've seen online, just input the code into the hub world rift.

BATTLE LAB

The Battle Lab disappeared for a little bit back in May but it's back (phew) and ready for us to dive right into. Battle Lab differs from Creative in that it is set on the same island as Battle Royale; you can just tweak with the game rules.

Battle Lab is a great way to put a little twist on the Battle Royale classic, but it's also a great opportunity to get familiar with the island without worrying about 99 other players (and some aggro wildlife) out there trying to take you out.

CREATE YOUR OWN BATTLE ROYALE:

In Battle Lab, you're creating your own game mode, not the arena. Epic helps you out by giving you access to existing LTM rules as a starting point, but you can customize other game options (everywhere from loot drops to fall damage and gravity effects), before inviting your friends to start the game and play by your rules... Or you could just dive in solo.

BATTLE LAB EXCLUSIVE:

This game mode has the same loot pool as Battle Royale, but it also has an exclusive item - Bot Grenades. These can be thrown to spawn either Friendly or Enemy bots. You can find them pretty much everywhere: on the ground, in chests, supply drops and llamas.

TIP:

If you're a Battle Royale newbie and a little nervous about dropping into the game and facing other players, Enemy Bots can be a good way to practice combat situations before trying a match. Sure, they can't replicate the playstyle of a human opponent, but they can be useful to familiarize yourself with weapon usage, combos and drills, like throwing them to the ground and practicing high ground shots.

PARTY ROYALE

You know, the world of Fortnite is pretty fun when you're not dodging headshots and rabid wildlife left, right and center. Sometimes it's fun just to run about without the looming dread of imminent death, and Party Royale is the perfect mode to do so. Chill out, catch a movie, dance at a concert or race some Quadcrashers - whatever you want to do, breathe easy and hop right onto the Party Island.

THE PARTY ISLAND

Party Royale takes place on an exclusive map that's different from the Battle Royale map. This island is purely for pleasure, and comes equipped with everything you need for your social Fortnite experience.

The Plaza: This is where you'll spawn, right in the middle of the island. Think of this like a hub, where you find

The Main Stage: This lies to the east of the island and plays host to the island's musical events (from Travis Scott to BTS) when they take place. From the Plaza, look out for SOFDEEZ ice-cream parlour - there are disco ball signs leading the way from there.

The Big Screen: This lies to the west of the island, and is the place to be if you want to catch exclusive videos and screenings (like Christopher Nolan's Fortnite Movie Nite, or Epic's animated Apple takedown). From the Plaza, take the bridge near the café and Peely's Banana Stand.

TAKE AIM

While Party Royale is a certified chill zone, it wouldn't be Fortnite without some form of wieldable gun, right? Luckily the weapons available in Party Royale can't deal any real damage, but they sure can cause a mess.

- Pick a team and start a paintball fight with the orange and purple Paint Grenades and Paint Launchers.

- Get ready to hurl some food through the air with zero consequences (finally, right?). Grab a Burger or Tomato and start a food fight.

- Or you know, you can always shoot a plunger at someone with a Plunger's Bow. Whatever floats your boat, bro.

TIP:

Want to change your skin before the big event? Don't worry about exiting out to the Locker in the Lobby - just hop into one of the blue phone booths around the island to change in Party Royale.

GAME ON

Even if there's not a big event scheduled, there's still plenty to do in Party Royale.

- Play a game of football at the Soccer Pitch (F3).
- Dabble in some boat racing at Fishstick's Boat Race (E7).
- Head over to Barnyard Obstacles (E6) for an obstacle time trial.
- Catch some air in your motorboat in the Flying Boat Atoll (B6).
- Go to Quadcrasher Motocross (C5) to race some classic Quadcrashers.
- Take on a nautical time trial at Buccaneer Bay (C2).

TIP:

Party Royale has its own set of emotes for you to hang out and interact with your friends. These emotes are exclusive to this mode, so make sure you check them out while you've got the chance!

FORTNITE COMPETITIVE

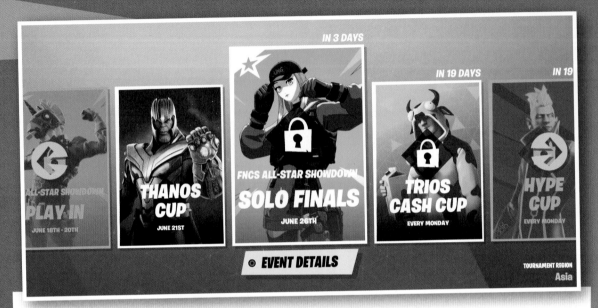

IN 3 DAYS

ALL-STAR SHOWDOWN
PLAY-IN
JUNE 18TH - 20TH

THANOS CUP
JUNE 21ST

FNCS ALL-STAR SHOWDOWN
SOLO FINALS
JUNE 26TH

IN 19 DAYS

TRIOS CASH CUP
EVERY MONDAY

IN 19

HYPE CUP
EVERY MONDAY

◉ **EVENT DETAILS**

TOURNAMENT REGION
Asia

The world of competitive gaming has had to undergo some serious changes over the last few years as LAN events became harder to stage and everything was forced to go online, but Epic took it all in their stride. While some scenes faltered, Fortnite kept going strong, with even more opportunities for everyone to dive in and make a name for themselves in Fortnite Competitive.

TIP:

Did you know that back in the 'glory days' of 2019, the Fortnite World Cup was one of the biggest gaming events in history, with over 2.3 million viewers online and almost 20,000 in attendance.

ENTER THE ARENA

So you want to test your might and see how you compare against other players? Then jump on into the Arena, pick your event and get ready to get hype - oh, my bad, Hype, like, literally get Hype, it's a currency

Get Hype: Hype isn't just a vibe, it's the competitive point system - your rank, effectively. Your Hype determines your Division, and earning Hype in Arena matches (the amount you earn is based on both your placement and eliminations) will let you climb from Open League right up to the Champion League.

Not sure where to start? Hype Nite is the most accessible of the competitive bouts, and geared towards lower-level players as it has a maximum Hype requirement of 1500 for entry. It's specifically designed to act as an entry point for anyone looking to venture into the competitive scene - this is where your competitive journey may just begin.

TIP:

2021 saw the competitive scene expand to include more collaboration competitions, like the Thanos Cup, the UEFA Euro 2020TM Cup and the console-exclusive Aloy Cup.

FORTNITE CHAMPION SERIES (FNCS)

FNCS is the most high profile ingame competitive event, and acts as a cadence for each competitive season. This series is the real deal - it even offers cash prizes for top-ranking competitors. And this is Epic we're talking about, so you know the cash prize is nothing to sneeze at. Chapter 2: Season 6's overall prize pool was a cool $3,000,000.

There's an open qualification system, but it's a three week affair spanning across global regions that is designed to truly separate the wheat from the chaff.

TIP:

Not interested in playing but curious to check it out? You can catch the major FNCS events on the big screen in Party Royale and cheer on the competitors ingame.

QUIZ ANSWERS

Did you take the quiz on p. 50-51? Hope you've made note of your answers, because it's time to total up your points and see how you scored, and most importantly, see how long you'll survive.

1. a) 3   b) 2   c) 2   d) 0
2. a) 1   b) 2   c) 3   d) 0
3. a) 1   b) 2   c) 3   d) 0
4. a) 3   b) 2   c) 0   d) 1
5. a) 3   b) 0   c) 0   d) 0
6. a) 1   b) 2   c) 0   d) 3
7. a) 0   b) 1   c) 2   d) 3
8. a) 1   b) 3   c) 2   d) 0
9. a) 3   b) 2   c) 0   d) 0
10. a) 2 b) 3   c) 1   d) 0

RESULTS

0-7 POINTS: YOU PLACED #100 - #75!

...Not the strongest of starts, sure, but there's always room for improvement. Looks like your fundamental knowledge isn't quite there yet, so maybe re-read (or read, be honest - you kinda skipped over the pages before, right?) if you want to place beyond the landing frenzy.

8-15 POINTS: YOU PLACED #74 - #50!

Not bad! There's a basic understanding of the game mechanics there, for sure, and while you'll likely make your way out of landing okay, you might struggle if you come across someone on your way into the eye. Have another look at our duelling tips and weapon guides for some finesse.

16-23 POINTS: YOU PLACED #49 - #25!

Almost there! You've got a sound grasp of the fundamentals and you're almost there - the devil's in the details when it comes to Fortnite, and there are a few finer points that you haven't quite got down yet. It's likely the numbers at this point, like knowing your healing efficiencies or mat robustness. You'll get it in no time.

24-30 POINTS: YOU PLACED TOP 25!

Okay, cue the applause, because it looks like someone (i.e. You, take a bow) has been paying attention! You've survived the landing frenzy, came out on top of encounters as you head towards the eye and know how to build your way out of nearly anything. A Victory Royale is well and truly in your grasp; the only thing that stands in your way is the knowledge of your opponents. There might be someone out there with just as much knowledge as you, but you'll always have the edge if you keep practicing (it makes perfect, so they say). Hope you've got an emote picked out for a post-kill corpse dance ready - it's only a matter of time.